THIS BOOK
BELONGS TO:

The Conner Family

St. Francis
and the Animals

Written by Alice Joyce Davidson

Illustrated by Maggie Swanson

Regina
Press

Francis of Assisi
had a very special love
for all of God's creation,
gifts from God above.

He thanked God for the sun, the moon,
the stars that filled the sky,
the valleys and the seas below
and hills that rose up high.

One day as he was traveling
the roadside filled with birds,
Francis gathered them around him
and preached these special words --

"Sister Birds, sing praise to God
for He has given you tall trees
to nest in, food to eat,
the joy of flying too."

Wild rabbits came to him
and felt his love and care.
Francis would protect them
and free them from a snare.

His brother lambs knew Francis
was a friend who loved them too,
for any time they needed help
he knew just what to do.

Francis heard about a wolf
who terrified a town.
"Brother Wolf, come here," he said.
The vicious wolf sat down.

"I know you're hungry but you must
control your killing ways.
Make peace and everybody here
will feed you all your days."

The wolf promised Francis
that he would hunt no more.
And Brother Wolf, from that day
on was fed from door to door.

Francis loved God's creatures,
the big ones and the small,
the wild ones and the meek ones too,
he thanked God for them all.

Francis taught us how to love
everything around us --
to care for trees, the land and seas
and God's gifts which surround us.

Thank you, God, for Brother sun
who gives us light each day.
And thank you, God, for Sister Earth
and all she brings our way.

Thank you, God, yes, thank you
for your gifts both great and small.
And thank you, too, for caring for
your creatures one and all.